Beyond
the Deception

Learning to
Defend the Truth

Dave Wager

Foreword by Rev. J. Michael Fox

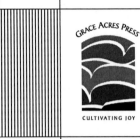

Grace Acres Press
P.O. Box 22
Larkspur, CO 80118
888-700-GRACE (4722)
(303) 681-9995
(303) 681-9996 fax
www.GraceAcresPress.com

Grace Acres Press also publishes books in a variety of
electronic formats. Some content that appears in print may
not be available in electronic books.

Throughout this book, we use the following abbreviations:

NIV *New International Version*

Scripture taken from the *Holy Bible, New International Version.*®
NIV.® Copyright © 1973, 1978, 1984 by International Bible
Society. Used by permission of Zondervan Publishing House.
All rights reserved.

NLT *New Living Testament*

Holy Bible, New Living Translation. Copyright © 1996
by Tyndale Charitable Trust. All rights reserved. Database
copyright © 1997 NavPress Software.

Library of Congress Cataloging-in-Publication Data:
Wager, Dave, 1956–
   Beyond the deception : learning to defend the truth / Dave
Wager.
       p.   cm. — (The intimate warrior series)
   ISBN: 978-1-60265-003-9
       1. Truthfulness and falsehood—Biblical teaching.
2. Truthfulness and falsehood—Religious aspects—Christianity—
Meditations. 3. Bible. N.T. Jude—Meditations. 4. Bible. N.T.
Peter, 2nd—Meditations. I. Title.
   BS2815.6.T78W34   2008
   242—dc22
                                                         2007047608

Printed in the United States of America
10 09 08   01 02 03 04 05 06 07 08 09 10

Praise for *Beyond the Deception*

If we are successfully to wage war against Satan, we must first understand his strategies. That's the last thing the devil wants, so I suspect that reading Dave Wager's book, Beyond the Deception, *is one of the last things Satan wants. Some people live their entire lives and never grasp the insights that Dave Wager shares here in pithy, easily read thoughts. They are like dynamite for destroying the devil's deception.*

> Dr. Woodrow Kroll
> President
> Back to the Bible International

Based on key New Testament passages, these are timely reminders about the importance of truth and our adversary who seeks to distort and deceive. This is a most useful study on a most important topic!

> Dr. Les Lofquist
> IFCA International
> Executive Director
> Grandville, Michigan

I have used it each morning since you sent it to me for my personal time of meeting with the Lord. It has been a personal challenge to focus on these Scriptures and thoughts and allow them to speak into my own life. As a mission's director and pastor to missionaries, I see this kind of guide as vital to keeping us on target. I am acutely interested in the spiritual development of our missionaries and this material is the kind I constantly look for. Dave Wager has a way of making us face the truth and ask the Lord "Where am I?" It is crucial that we, as Christ followers, continue to grow and stay in tune with the Lord and recognize anything that would throw us off. It is this type of thought-provoking

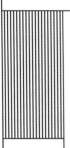

*reading that I, myself, need to read and re-read to keep
checking on my own spiritual authenticity.*

HARRY R. (BOB) MOYER III
South America Mission, Inc.
Associate Director for the Fields

---

*With his third installment Wager enables readers to uncover
many of the deceptions often used by the enemy. He offers
a poignant reminder to all to be on the lookout for those,
both inside and outside the church, who seek to distort our
perceptions, and shows how we can expose their lies
through the illuminating light of clearly presented biblical
truths. His concise dissection of Scripture is remarkable
because it not only reveals the warning signs in those
around us, but also challenges each of us to take a closer
look at our own lives.*

STEVE CURRINGTON
Founder, Reformers Unanimous

---

*Dave's heart for God and his passion for the truth have
been, and will continue to be, a help to many.*

DAVID JOHNSON, Senior Pastor,
Church of the Open Door, Minnesota

---

*I have always admired Dave's ability to step back, look
critically at himself, and "do something" about it. Upon
such transparent honesty does this book motivate action in
the reader to combat the deception and distortion of truth.
Dave has truly integrated his upbringing, his faith, and his
football life lessons into becoming a down-to-earth warrior*

for his God against the resistance of Satan. I have not met an individual more realistic and humble about his own human fallibility; hence Dave's dedication to knowing God and seeking His will and direction. Dave's challenge is to focus so intently on God's plan that any difficulty, pain, or suffering for God becomes just an obstacle to be defeated, just as the opposition or hard training in sports must be defeated or overcome to reach success. You will be convinced to seek, know, and defend the truth.

NANCY SWIDER-PELTZ
Four-time Olympian, world
record holder, coach

Fundamental and vital to the Christian walk are the thoughts shared in this book. Dave uses passion, clarity, and scripturally sound encouragement to help us walk in the grace of God. I highly recommend this book to all who desire to worship the Lord in spirit and in truth.

GREG BUCHANAN
Gospel harpist, California

In a day when absolute truth is being questioned by so many people, it is refreshing to read Beyond the Deception. He has captured the meaning of real truth. With his life experiences and the puzzle illustrations, this is must reading for every Christian.

REV. DEAN B. YODER
President and CEO
Christian World Outreach

As thieves when they would rob a man draw him aside out of the highway into some wood, and then cut his throat, so this grand deceiver and his agents draw men aside from the right way of God's worship into some bypaths of error to their ruin. The devil he is the cheater of cheaters, and deluder of deluders; it is his constant trade, as the participle implies. And this is the reason why many false teachers may die with boldness and courage for their opinions, viz., because they are blinded and deluded by the devil; they think themselves martyrs, when they are grand deceivers and grossly deceived. We had need, therefore, to pray for the Spirit of grace and illumination that we may see the methods, depths, and devices of Satan and avoid them.

T. Hall, B. D.

This book is dedicated to my daughters, Krista and Sara Wager, and to those in their generation who are willing to evaluate their lives on the truth of God's Word. It is my profound hope and prayer that young people from their generation will begin—and continue—to live in a way that exposes the lies of Satan while revealing the truths of Scripture.

Contents

Acknowledgments

I remain forever grateful for the truths that God reveals through His Word by His Spirit. Deception is the greatest tool of the evil one, in that when we are deceived, we do not know we are wrong. God's Word alone has the capability of cutting through what we think and allows us to evaluate our thoughts and ideas on something that is absolute and unchanging.

It is for this reason that I would like to acknowledge those old heroes of the faith: Elijah, David, Daniel, Joseph, Moses, Joshua, Noah, and the others mentioned in Hebrews chapter 11; and the 400 people and their families who will be martyred today because of their faithfulness to the King and His truth. Those heroes thought it more important to die acknowledging the truth than to live a lie.

May all who know Christ live and die in the truths that He has revealed. We indeed have a cloud of witnesses who are "cheering" us on.

About the Author

For the past twenty-five years, Dave Wager has served as a leader, friend, and teacher to thousands who have entered the educational grounds of Silver Birch Ranch in White Lake, Wisconsin. Today Dave continues to serve as the president of Silver Birch Ranch, and also teaches at camps, conferences, churches, and businesses throughout the world.

Dave's life has been dedicated to the growth of young people, first as a volunteer youth worker and then later as a fifth-grade teacher. He has served as president of the Wisconsin Christian Camping Association and currently teaches a class in "Christian Life and Ethics" at the Nicolet Bible Institute. Dave holds a B.A. from Wheaton College and an M.S. Ed. from Northern Illinois University.

Dave desires that each person he meets walk intimately with God and fulfill the purposes for which he or she was designed. He believes that joy and effectiveness in life, work, and ministry come from knowing what really matters. His focus is in examining how today's choices affect the real bottom line: knowing what we are about, what are our responsibilities, and what are God's responsibilities.

Foreword

It has been my pleasure and joy to have known Dave Wager for many years. While in high school, I was his Sunday school teacher—Dave was probably about eight years old. Through the years I have watched Dave develop and grow into a fine man of character and experience. Therefore, I eagerly read this book, and find in it both a refreshing candor and a strong biblical foundation.

I have no doubt concerning God's design and desire for each of His children. He deeply longs for us to know victory, peace, and contentment in Him and His ways. As we obediently seek to follow Him, we will find our enemy all the more eager to deceive and destroy us. In this volume, Dave makes it clear that Satan has a strategy of failure for each believer. Some are subtle, whereas others are blatant and brassy. The enemy can defeat the ignorant believer, but he cannot overcome the Christian who knows the Word of God and understands the mission and purpose of God. Dave reminds us that Satan is "no match for Jesus . . . and he should be no match for us who are in Christ Jesus."

I am convinced that you, too, will be encouraged and informed as you read this volume. Dave writes, "It is so easy to make excuses for my lack of service of effectiveness. I so often want to say that I would do better if I could speak better, had more education, or had a few

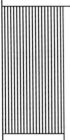

more resources so I could share a little more. I am plainly deceived [by the enemy] when I think that I will be used of God someday when I gain something that He can use. God uses what is available: those who are intimate with Him, those who make themselves useable vessels." Through the writings of Peter, God teaches us that He has given His born-again children everything needed for living a godly life in this world.

As is his style, Dave is careful to lace the book with examples from real lives, like those of Moses, David, Peter, and even the Lord Jesus. Bless the Lord, He has crafted His own children with "no parts missing." I wholeheartedly recommend this valuable and insightful book to your reading and as a reference for life. Blessings on Dave Wager for his practical and Scriptural help in the face of devilish deception and fraud.

November 2007   Rev. J. Michael Fox
                                   Hebrews 12:1, 2
                                   Child Evangelism Fellowship
                                   Will County Chapter
                                   Crest Hill, Illinois

Introduction

One day I found a jigsaw puzzle piece lying on my desk. I knew that I had used the idea of a jigsaw puzzle before, in attempting to explain how one particular something fits into the whole, so to see this piece lying on my desk was no big deal. That is, until I started looking at this little piece. As I looked at it, I began to wonder.

I wondered about the picture of which this was a part. I tried to decide or imagine what the picture was, but no matter how hard I tried, I couldn't figure it out. I just didn't have enough information.

I then began to wonder how many pieces of this puzzle I was missing. Was this a puzzle containing a hundred pieces, two hundred pieces, or a thousand pieces? I didn't know. Once again, I was frustrated by a lack of information. Actually, I was getting totally frustrated because there was really no way to find the answer. The box cover was long gone, and half of the pieces of this puzzle were missing. I wasn't even certain that the piece I had found belonged in the bag of pieces I had on my shelf.

I was frustrated not just because of the puzzle piece, but also because of what this reminded me about life. So often I try to understand the universe by approaching things from my own perspective, my own experiences, and my own knowledge. I so often forget that I am a very little cog in a very large wheel, and that there is a lot of

history, a lot of future, and a lot of people that are not factored into my understanding of life and death.

I have concluded that trying to figure out life is like trying to figure out the number of pieces or the picture a puzzle will create without having the box to refer to. The best I can do is guess.

I then began to wonder about life. Is guessing really the best I can do in relation to what is good and bad, right and wrong? Must I make decisions, or *do* I make decisions, based on my minute scrap of understanding, my single puzzle piece? If I do, how often am I wrong?

I have realized that I must often ask the One who made the puzzle for information about how the pieces fit together. I constantly need to go to the One who knows, the One who has been through it all, and ask Him to guide my very understanding of things, so that I can put thoughts, ideas, and actions into their proper place.

I am not the One who made it all, sees it all, or has experienced it all—but I can be intimate with the One who did, has, and is.

Truth today seems hard to find, yet it has never been easier to come by. Truth is hard to recognize because we often allow too many voices to define it for us. There is only One voice that is definitive when it comes to truth, and that is the very voice of God. As we open His Word and read what He says, truth becomes obvious.

As I spend time with God, the puzzle piece of life He has given to me begins to make sense. I begin to see what the larger picture looks like and how I fit into the whole. I begin to be challenged by truth, rather than by the fool's task of making it up.

Satan's greatest tool is deception. He is shrewd and works us over by using our ignorance, ego, curiosity, and senses to create what we may easily mistake for truth. In some cases, we are so deceived that we stop looking for truth, and thereafter we simply fill our lives with unimportant nothings, finding others to confirm what we believe. It is time for us to move beyond the deception, and instead gain our understanding and live our lives in the realm of truth.

It is my hope and desire that this book helps you to see truth and make adjustments to the truth as God reveals it to you. We must not put all our time and energy into the pursuit of the new, while the true sits by unnoticed. If grasped and heeded, truth is yet ready and willing to sculpt positive changes in our lives and culture.

Thought for Day 1

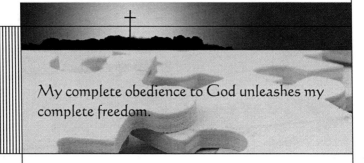

My complete obedience to God unleashes my complete freedom.

Jude 1:3–4 (NLT)

3 Dear friends, I had been eagerly planning to write to you about the salvation we all share. But now I find that I must write about something else, urging you to defend the faith that God has entrusted once for all time to his holy people.

4 I say this because some ungodly people have wormed their way into your churches, saying that God's marvelous grace allows us to live immoral lives. The condemnation of such people was recorded long ago, for they have denied our only Master and Lord, Jesus Christ.

Are there false teachers in my church? What do they look like? What do they sound like?

Satan is good at what he does, and it seems that he has planted his covert agents within the power structure of the local church. For these people to thrive, they need an environment that will allow their ideas to grow and slowly take over the very thought processes of the unsuspecting.

The book of Jude gives us insights into what these people look like, what they say, and what is important to them. I need to be careful, as I read this book of Scripture, not

just to be on the lookout for those who are characterized by Jude, but to ask if I, too, exhibit some of these dangerous characteristics.

The first trait seems evident. Those who are deceived, those who are false teachers, have never really grasped the true meaning of salvation. When we place our trust in Christ, we are not just saved from an eternity in Hell. We are not just saved to be with Christ in Heaven. The fact is that our salvation allows us to live different lives now! Our salvation has freed us from the penalty of our sins; it has freed us from the power of sin in our lives today; and it will, one day, free us from the very presence of sin.

False teachers do not understand this. In fact, they live lives that are no different from those in the non-Christian world around them. When they are confronted, they talk of God's grace as if His grace were a license for evil. These false teachers may talk about the importance of "relating" to a non-Christian world in order to reach nonbelievers with the Gospel, but the gospel of which they speak has no transformative power. It is not the Gospel of Christ; rather, it is the good news of self-centeredness, of self-absorption, and of attempting to make this type of lifestyle acceptable, or even admirable, to God.

The first and most important characteristic to recognize in a false teacher is the justification of sin. Sin is never acceptable to one who truly loves God. One who claims that the grace of God excuses sinful behavior, and who encourages others to believe the same and continue in their sinful ways, is doing the work of Satan, not of God.

Where do you stand? Do you really hate sin, or do you make provision and excuses for it? Do you listen to people who justify their actions, or to those who recognize evil and cry out to God for mercy as they move away from evil? We are warned about false teachers because they do exist. *God, help me know that I am not one of them!*

Another Piece of the Truth Puzzle

Freedom comes from obedience. Obedience comes from the fear of God. The fear of God comes from knowing God.

_____

_____

_____

_____

_____

_____

_____

_____

_____

_____

_____

_____

Thought for Day 2

God is love . . . and holy, and righteous,
and a judge, ...

Jude 1:5–7 (NLT)

5 So I want to remind you, though you already know these things, that Jesus first rescued the nation of Israel from Egypt, but later he destroyed those who did not remain faithful.

6 And I remind you of the angels who did not stay within the limits of authority God gave them but left the place where they belonged. God has kept them securely chained in prisons of darkness, waiting for the great day of judgment.

7 And don't forget Sodom and Gomorrah and their neighboring towns, which were filled with immorality and every kind of sexual perversion. Those cities were destroyed by fire and serve as a warning of the eternal fire of God's judgment.

"I want to remind you . . . " "I remind you . . . "
"And don't forget . . . . "

Jude is careful to show us that the false teachers among us are those who choose to forget that God is not one-dimensional. In fact, these false teachers often talk about a God who will forgive, a God who will show mercy, a God who certainly would understand our sin, and who is willing to forgive our sins. This is all true and should not

be minimized; however, we need to recognize that God is also a God who judges, and this must be a part of our discussion too.

False teachers want to believe only what they find acceptable about God, and want to ignore what they struggle with. Like it or not, the facts in the Bible are clear: God is love, and desires all men to come to repentance. Those who do not come to repentance will die, having wasted their lives, and they will be punished in Hell for eternity. Those who want to run from God will face the wrath of God. Those who choose to live self-centered, egotistical lives will pay the price.

Many look at salvation as a ticket to Heaven, but you could just as easily look at it as a way to escape the wrath of God.

During my college days, I played defensive end for Wheaton College. On the field, I was focused on the game of football. Off the field, I was focused on my studies. In my junior year, I met a person who became a friend. After we had been friends for a while, this person told me that who I was was much different from what many thought of me. I was told that I had a reputation for being a wild man, a killer of sorts, a focused mean machine. Indeed, I probably was that way on the football field, but the football field was only one part of my life. I also volunteered my summers at a youth camp, worked with eight-year-old boys at our local church, and volunteered to clean our church. I was an elementary education major and was constantly working in the local school systems.

To know me, you needed to see more of me than my Saturday-afternoon football escapades. To know God, we

need to see God's gracious and merciful side, as well as His judging, justice-dealing side.

God will punish evil. God will send those who reject Christ to Hell. God will, in the end, be exalted as God. These truths must be balanced with the knowledge that God desires all men to experience His mercy, and invites them to salvation.

Which of God's characteristics do I focus on, to the exclusion of others? Why?

Another Piece of the Truth Puzzle

God is love and will judge, punish, reward, and rule the universe in the context of true love. Love is defined by God. God is not defined by love.

_____

_____

_____

_____

_____

_____

_____

_____

Thought for Day 3

God is God, I am Dave. This actually means something.

Jude 1:8–10 (NLT)

8 In the same way, these people — who claim authority from their dreams — live immoral lives, defy authority, and scoff at supernatural beings.

9 But even Michael, one of the mightiest of the angels, did not dare accuse the devil of blasphemy, but simply said, "The Lord rebuke you!" (This took place when Michael was arguing with the devil about Moses' body.)

10 But these people scoff at things they do not understand. Like unthinking animals, they do whatever their instincts tell them, and so they bring about their own destruction.

I once was asked to speak to several pastors, many of whom no longer used the Bible as the foundation for their messages. Instead, because of time constraints, they relied on their dreams. In a strange way, they thought this made them the final authority on spiritual matters: They believed that their dreams were from God, and that anything they dreamed would certainly be worthy of teaching to others.

Satan is alive and well and fears only one thing: the Word of God. It is with the Word of God that Satan is

defeated. Satan cannot stand against what God says. Though I may speak and think as cleverly and powerfully as I possibly can, Satan can out-talk me and out-think me every time. If God says something, though, Satan is helpless, defeated, and rendered powerless.

Satan will do whatever it takes to make sure that people are not in God's Word. He knows that God's Word alone will expose the satanic methods, and that it is God's Word that will give power to the powerless.

There are some today who minimize the enemy—to the enemy's delight. Because they do not understand how Satan works, they decide that they have figured out how he *must* work, and they live their lives in the arena of their understanding rather than in the arena of truth. They begin to scoff at those who cling to the truth, calling them narrow-minded, legalistic, and even fundamentalists. What they are really doing is exalting their minds, their thinking, and their way of life. They are really saying, "If I do not understand it, it cannot be," and thereby they seek to reduce God and the unseen realm to what they find understandable.

Those who live by their own understanding are false teachers, for we are told much that goes way beyond our understanding. Those who live by their own understanding live their lives by instinct rather than by wisdom.

Instinct instructs us to satisfy our urges and justify our desires. Wisdom dictates prudence in actions, obedience over understanding, and faith over fear.

God does not need you to understand His ways to be God or to be right. God need not justify anything to you or me to be right. God is God, and I am Dave. God is and has always been. I once was not. God is the creator. I am the created.

I need to act in the context of these realities, not in the context of my own understanding. God, *help me get to the point where my obedience is more important than my understanding!*

Another Piece of the Truth Puzzle

God has always been and will be forever. I once was not, but now will be forever. Real understanding must come from God, not from me.

_____

_____

_____

_____

_____

_____

_____

_____

_____

_____

_____

_____

_____

_____

_____

_____

_____

_____

_____

_____

_____

_____

_____

_____

_____

_____

_____

_____

_____

_____

_____

Thought for Day 4

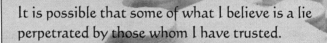

It is possible that some of what I believe is a lie perpetrated by those whom I have trusted.

Jude 1:12–16 (NLT)

12 When these people eat with you in your fellowship meals commemorating the Lord's love, they are like dangerous reefs that can shipwreck you. They are like shameless shepherds who care only for themselves. They are like clouds blowing over the land without giving any rain. They are like trees in autumn that are doubly dead, for they bear no fruit and have been pulled up by the roots.

13 They are like wild waves of the sea, churning up the foam of their shameful deeds. They are like wandering stars, doomed forever to blackest darkness.

14 Enoch, who lived in the seventh generation after Adam, prophesied about these people. He said, "Listen! The Lord is coming with countless thousands of his holy ones

15 to execute judgment on the people of the world. He will convict every person of all the ungodly things they have done and for all the insults that ungodly sinners have spoken against him."

16 THESE PEOPLE ARE GRUMBLERS AND COMPLAINERS, LIVING ONLY TO SATISFY THEIR DESIRES. THEY BRAG LOUDLY ABOUT THEMSELVES, AND THEY FLATTER OTHERS TO GET WHAT THEY WANT.

False teachers, or deceived teachers, are those who have wormed their way into our lives, our churches, and our families and teach us things about life, God, and eternity that sound good, but are not true. They are like unseen reefs in the sea that destroy unsuspecting ships.

This is the problem. Many of those who are false teachers—those among us who are being used by Satan—are really quite good at what they do and are well hidden. In fact, we may think it's fine to share our "sea" with them, until we actually come into full contact with them and the teaching they spread. Those who are false teachers have a following of people whose lives seem to be forever in disaster. False teachers are not really interested in the good of the people; they are interested only in their own good. They teach for what they get out of it. They give for what they get out of it. They love for what they get out of it. They serve for what they get out of it. They lead for what they get out of it. If they got nothing out of it, they would soon be gone, because to them, any sacrifice is, well, unacceptable.

Since this is the case, they often flatter others, or use others to accomplish their goals. Their pragmatic ministry is based on the latest business practices, and their structures are aimed more toward getting people on board than toward developing people of character.

As I travel, I often listen to Christian or public radio stations. Many times, both of these types of stations are on the air due to the generosity of donors, and we are often reminded of how dependent they are on us, the listeners. It is very interesting that most of the time we are encouraged to give because of what we receive. We receive a blessing, and if we want to continue to receive this blessing, we must sacrificially give.

How interesting. I should sacrificially give for, well, . . . for me! What a grand idea to propagate. What a new twist on the old idea of giving because God has placed a burden on your heart to give. What an acceptable deception!

Why do I teach? Why do I lead? Why do I give? *God, help me to be honest in my answers!*

Another Piece of the Truth Puzzle

It is possible that what I do can be disguised in a way that makes it seem like I am doing it for someone else or for some noble cause, when in reality my "good works" are another expression of my self-centeredness.

_____

_____

_____

_____

_____

Thought for Day 5

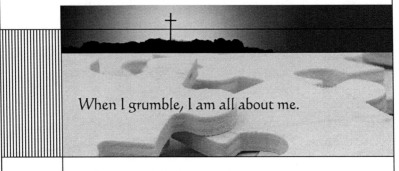

When I grumble, I am all about me.

Jude 1:16 (NLT)

16 THESE PEOPLE ARE GRUMBLERS AND COMPLAINERS, LIVING ONLY TO SATISFY THEIR DESIRES. THEY BRAG LOUDLY ABOUT THEMSELVES, AND THEY FLATTER OTHERS TO GET WHAT THEY WANT.

What would God say characterizes my life? Am I one who is thankful? Do I have genuine joy?

It is often said that the squeaky wheel gets the grease. We have learned this behavior by being in society, and we use it often because it works.

Whatever happened to those who were silent before the Lord? What happens to those who wait patiently on the Lord? What happens if we sit still and know that God is God? What will happen to us?

How powerful are the circumstances in my life when it comes to dictating joy and peace?

False teachers are really all about themselves and enhancing whatever is important to them. If fame is important, they search for the spotlight. If fortune is important, they search for the pot of gold. If health and beauty are important, they search for the fountain

of youth. If satisfying urges is important, they search for their next "urge fix."

What is important to God? I do not mean to ask what God may be interested in, for He is interested in all aspects of my life. I am asking: What is *really* important to *God*?

Is my comfort really that important to Him? Is my health really that important to Him? How about my wealth; is that what is important to Him?

What is it that God is trying to accomplish? Would He use my reputation to accomplish it? Would He use my health? My wealth? My comfort?

If so, and if God is actually in charge of things, why would I complain if He chooses to use my health to bring our world to Him? Why would I moan when I get the privilege of using my resources to help the needy, or to further Kingdom work? Why would I complain when I am mistreated, if God uses this mistreatment to His honor and glory?

I would complain because I am not connected to what God is doing. I would complain because I am self-absorbed. My moaning and groaning in life imply either that God is not good or that He is not sovereign. Neither of these statements is true, for God is indeed good and sovereign. Therefore, my perspective is skewed.

I need to start acting in a way that demonstrates God's goodness and sovereignty, or face the reality of being one of the false teachers who will one day be strictly judged for behavior not befitting a true teacher.

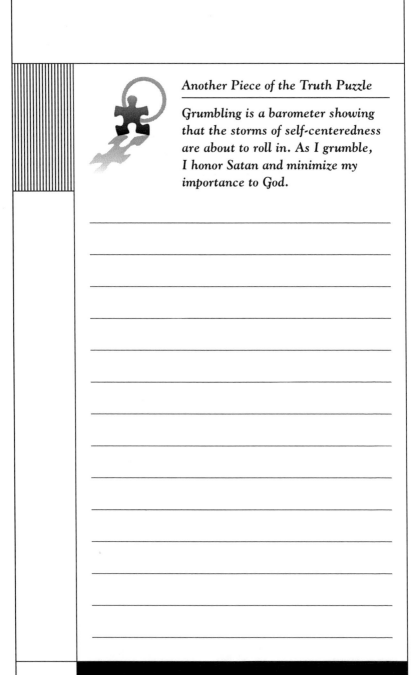

Another Piece of the Truth Puzzle

Grumbling is a barometer showing that the storms of self-centeredness are about to roll in. As I grumble, I honor Satan and minimize my importance to God.

Thought for Day 6

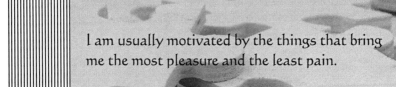

I am usually motivated by the things that bring me the most pleasure and the least pain.

Jude 1:17–19

17 But you, my dear friends, must remember what the apostles of our Lord Jesus Christ said.

18 They told you that in the last times there would be scoffers whose purpose in life is to satisfy their ungodly desires.

19 These people are the ones who are creating divisions among you. They follow their natural instincts because they do not have God's Spirit in them.

What is my purpose in life? I do not mean what is my *academic* purpose, but what is my God-given purpose?

The answer to this question is critical, for one day I will be judged upon this purpose. Jesus told the people that if they wanted to be His disciples, they must pick up their crosses daily and follow Him. The cross was Jesus' purpose, the reason He came to be and to die. He was so focused on this purpose that nothing could stop Him.

In fact, not long before Jesus was going to go to the cross, He prayed and asked God if there was any other way. There was not, so Jesus pressed on to accomplish what God put Him on earth to accomplish.

Satan worked overtime trying to get Jesus to give in to His fleshly desires. Satan tried again and again to get Him to abandon His purpose. Satan was no match for Jesus, though, and he should be no match for us who are in Christ Jesus.

In most cases, people are deceived into believing that their lives are about staying alive until they die. In most cases, people's goals have to do with self, not with the plans of God. In most cases, without even trying, people render themselves useless to the King and His purposes, because to achieve the purposes they were created to achieve, they must stay focused on the goal, even while the masses around them try to get them to loosen up and live for the moment.

Those who live their lives with the goal of having no regrets set their sights on the very purpose God created them to fulfill. Years ago, it became popular to talk about a God who did not make humans with specific purposes. In fact, it became popular to talk about doing whatever you liked, whatever brought you the most joy, whatever fulfilled you the most; supposedly, God would just bless your activities, as long as you loved Him and wanted His name to be known.

I am not certain what the thousands of martyrs throughout history would say of such a philosophy. To follow what is right, you must expose what is evil. When you expose evil, evil fights back.

In the Bible, the majority is usually wrong. Truth can never be dictated by the masses, for it already exists. Your purpose is given to you by God, even though Satan would love to deceive you into believing that any old purpose will do.

God is not random, and His plans are not fluid. He made you for a purpose, and He alone can reveal and equip you for that purpose. He must, for when you are in His plan, you will be vehemently opposed.

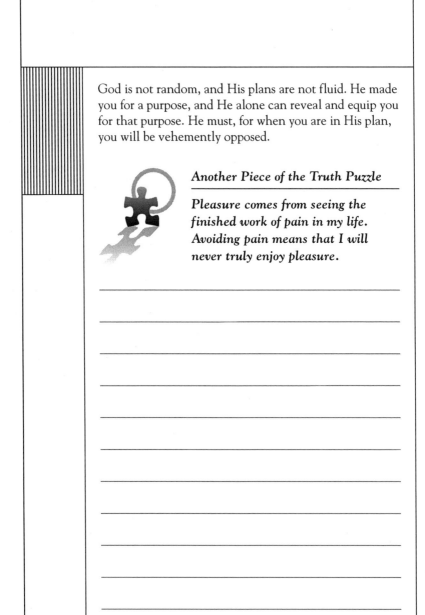

Another Piece of the Truth Puzzle

Pleasure comes from seeing the finished work of pain in my life. Avoiding pain means that I will never truly enjoy pleasure.

_____

_____

_____

_____

_____

_____

_____

_____

_____

_____

_____

Thought for Day 7

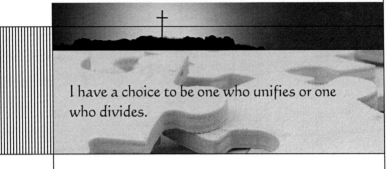

I have a choice to be one who unifies or one who divides.

Jude 1:19 (NLT)

19 THESE PEOPLE ARE THE ONES WHO ARE CREATING DIVISIONS AMONG YOU. THEY FOLLOW THEIR NATURAL INSTINCTS BECAUSE THEY DO NOT HAVE GOD'S SPIRIT IN THEM.

Those who cause divisions are those whom Satan is using to maximize his efforts. In fact, in many cases, there are so many divisions in the body of Christ that we cannot even recognize the body.

One of the unique features of Christianity is unity in diversity. What we have really turned that into is unity in nondiversity, which isn't really anything special at all. For example, if I surround myself with people who think like me, act like me, and have the same desires as me, and talk of how unified we are, I am talking of no great or unusual thing. If, however, I can describe a unity that comes when those around me are of different thoughts, ideas, and personalities, that is quite an achievement.

I think that there are far too many churches in the world. We tend to create new churches and fill them with like-minded people and then brag of our unity, when in reality it is disunity that has caused our church to exist in the first place.

Within the church, there is always a structure. With the new emphasis on self, our churches have become increasingly democratic in style, leading to endless discussions and opportunities to divide. Majority rule has become the litmus test for the will of God, and politics has overrun true leadership.

What we have is churches that, if they are not divided today, will be tomorrow, for the system promotes division instead of unity. It is not as if the church is being divided over doctrinal issues. Instead, the church is being divided over petty matters like the use or kind of music, the budget, how so-and-so was treated, whether the pastor is pastoral enough, and so on and so forth.

The bottom line throughout the Scriptures remains that those who are willing to divide the true body are not of God. This does not mean that we do not hold to true doctrine, for indeed we must. If the church is divided because of a stand on what is right, so be it. That is God's problem and He is capable of dealing with it. If we divide the church based on anything else, then we must be ready to answer to God for using whatever power and influence we had to destroy rather than to build up.

When I was much younger in ministry, my wise father told me that I should make sure I know what the basics of our faith really are—that is, the foundation of our faith—and never move from what is right. He also told me that I must be able to differentiate what is foundational truth from what are methods that might be used to convey this truth. He told me to cling tenaciously to the foundational truth, but to constantly challenge the methods. This has been most valuable advice.

Are you a uniter or a divider? Do you know what is worth fighting for and what should be challenged? Are you living in the truth, or are you being deceived?

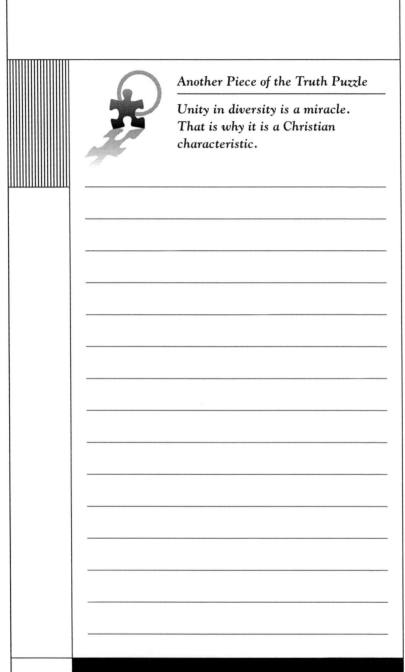

Another Piece of the Truth Puzzle

Unity in diversity is a miracle.
That is why it is a Christian
characteristic.

Thought for Day 8

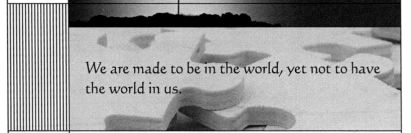

We are made to be in the world, yet not to have the world in us.

Jude 1:20–23 (NLT)

20 But you, dear friends, must build each other up in your most holy faith, pray in the power of the Holy Spirit,

21 and await the mercy of our Lord Jesus Christ, who will bring you eternal life. In this way, you will keep yourselves safe in God's love.

22 And you must show mercy to those whose faith is wavering.

23 Rescue others by snatching them from the flames of judgment. Show mercy to still others, but do so with great caution, hating the sins that contaminate their lives.

Jude finally gives me something to focus on that will help ensure that I am not counted among the false teachers. I am to focus on building up others' faith. I am to be one who obeys God and thereby unleashes the power of the Holy Spirit. I need to anticipate God's eventual mercy toward me, while I demonstrate His mercy to others. I need to live in such a way that other people are led to the King, while at the same time not being contaminated by the lives they lead.

This is easier said than done.

When you see a ship in dry dock, you know there is a problem. A ship was meant to be in the water, not on dry land. In fact, great efforts are made to ensure that a ship can stay in the water by making sure that the water surrounding the ship has no way to get into it.

Those who are true Christians were made by God to be in the world, but they were not made to allow the world into them. We are to be people who immerse ourselves in a pagan culture, while at the same time doing whatever it takes to maintain the seals that keep the water out of our hulls.

Years ago, I had an old fishing boat that had numerous leaks. The boat was given to me to enjoy, and the thought of spending hours on the lake fishing was splendid indeed. At first, the boat was magnificent. I did not mind the bailing, because I was so thrilled to be able to fish. It did not take long, though, before this bailing routine started to get old. Boats are made to float. They are made to keep the water out, and when water gets in, we spend our time bailing instead of sailing. Before long, I was looking for a way to get rid of the boat. The bailing got to me, I was discouraged, and I actually began to hate what I had once enjoyed.

Life is no different. God made us to be in the world to show the world who He is and to bring all men to repentance. Yet, if we have slow leaks that allow the world into us, we need to deal with those leaks, or face a future of discouragement and despair, for we will be constantly bailing in our lives, instead of sailing as God created us to.

What "seals" in your life should be in place? What are you allowing in that is taking too much time and robbing you of the joy of sailing through life? God did not mean for you to spend your time bailing. He indeed wants you to be sailing!

Another Piece of the Truth Puzzle

I can spend my time trying to "bail" my life's ship, or I can enjoy the journey. For now, the choice is mine.

_____

_____

_____

_____

_____

_____

_____

_____

_____

_____

_____

_____

_____

Thought for Day 9

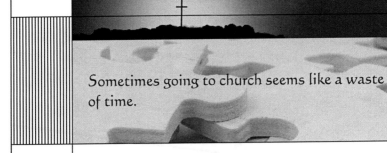

Sometimes going to church seems like a waste of time.

Titus 3:9–11 (NLT)

9 Do not get involved in foolish discussions about spiritual pedigrees or in quarrels and fights about obedience to Jewish laws. These things are useless and a waste of time.

10 If people are causing divisions among you, give a first and second warning. After that, have nothing more to do with them.

11 For people like that have turned away from the truth, and their own sins condemn them.

Certainly the early church was much tougher on its members than we are today. Perhaps the early church thought it had something to guard, something that was really special that needed protection. Perhaps the early church was focused and functional and wanted to keep it that way.

It seems so easy to get into endless discussions about things that are relatively unimportant. We can talk about our spiritual pedigrees, or how we believe in giving 15 percent of our income to the church rather than only 10 percent, and in the end we accomplish nothing concerning Kingdom purposes.

The fact is that much of what goes on in most churches is a waste of time. We gather a group of people in beautiful buildings and give them songs and speeches they like to hear. When things start to get personal, we get angry and try to make things more to our liking, more generic. We talk of tolerance, love, and mercy as if they were licenses for sin and stupidity. In some respects, we have turned the church into nothing more than a Christian United Nations assembly, where we are trying to achieve peace on earth by gaining the consensus of humanity, rather than invoking, following, and trusting in the power of God.

Much of our discussions are a waste of time and only widen the divisions within the true church. It is interesting that Paul warns Titus against such people, who are so into personal agendas and interpretations that they end up dividing the troops. He tells Titus to warn them several times, but also commands Titus to have nothing more to do with them when it becomes evident that they will not listen.

This sounds harsh, yet the church is not a political machine; it is the body of Christ on earth. We are not about the unimportant; we are about the most important. The sad reality is that most people will not even recognize the dividers in a church, for they have come to accept such behavior as the norm.

What is your church really about? What difference would it make if the doors of your church were closed? How would the purposes of the King be hampered because you no longer existed?

People with personal agendas not driven by the Holy Spirit should not be driving the purposes, plans, and procedures of our churches. I recently read some survey results about what is going on in local churches. It seems, at least according to those results, that 92 percent of people who claim to be born-again believers do not live according to a Christian worldview.

Those who live this way are dividing our churches, and they must either repent or be removed if our churches are to become a mighty force in God's hands again.

Where are you? What is going on in your church?

Another Piece of the Truth Puzzle

The body parts are useful only if they are in total and immediate obedience to the signal from the brain. Observing other body parts is not as important as responding to the brain.

_____

_____

_____

_____

_____

_____

_____

_____

Thought for Day 10

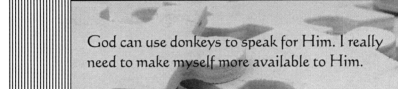

God can use donkeys to speak for Him. I really need to make myself more available to Him.

2 Peter 1:3–4 (NLT)

3 By his divine power, God has given us everything we need for living a godly life. We have received all of this by coming to know him, the one who called us to himself by means of his marvelous glory and excellence.

4 And because of his glory and excellence, he has given us great and precious promises. These are the promises that enable you to share his divine nature and escape the world's corruption caused by human desires.

We have received everything we need for living a godly life by coming to know God.

Imagine that. God actually has given me what I need. I really do not need a computer to live a godly life, or money, or a nice home, or power, or fancy clothes, or anything else. God is the One who equips me, and He does so as I seek Him.

It is so easy to make excuses for my lack of service of effectiveness. I so often want to say that I would do better if I could speak better, had more education, or had a few more resources so I could share a little more. I am plainly

deceived when I think that I will be used of God someday when I gain something that He can use. God uses what is available: those who are intimate with Him, those who make themselves useable vessels.

When Jesus fed the five thousand, He used the loaves and fishes of a little boy. When people came to Jesus with nothing but faith, when all they could do was squeeze though a crowd and touch his garment, that was all that was necessary.

God does the impossible. He just asks us, of our own free will, to place ourselves in a position He can use. When you think about the many He used in Scripture, you stand awed at the wonderful things He accomplished with such ungifted, untalented, unexceptional individuals. Moses was an abandoned child who did not seem gifted in leadership, yet he led and is considered one of the greatest leaders in history. David was a little shepherd boy. Daniel and his buddies were captured and put through a brainwashing program. Paul, the man who wrote much of the New Testament under the influence of the Holy Spirit, was the chief of all sinners.

There was a time when God brought water out of a rock. There was a time when God used a donkey to speak for Him. God has no need of my talent or ability, yet He desires my intimacy and obedience.

I am certain that I could be more effective in changing the world if I were more talented, if I had a higher profile, and if I had a better command of the English language—but those are all excuses, a deceptive smoke-screen eagerly supplied by Satan himself. God can and will use me as I know Him, love Him, and make myself available to Him.

I am most thankful that He did not leave the effectiveness of the ministry up to me.

Another Piece of the Truth Puzzle

I do not create the plan of God, nor vote on His plan. I am not one that can make anything good happen. It is a privilege to be used of and by Him, not a burden.

_____

_____

_____

_____

_____

_____

_____

_____

_____

_____

_____

_____

_____

Thought for Day 11

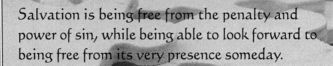

Salvation is being free from the penalty and power of sin, while being able to look forward to being free from its very presence someday.

2 Peter 1:5 (NLT)

5 In view of all this, make every effort to respond to God's promises. Supplement your faith with a generous provision of moral excellence, and moral excellence with knowledge . . .

So often we are deceived into believing that once we place our faith in Christ, we need not do anything else. This may be partly true, in that our salvation comes solely from our faith in Christ alone, but salvation is much more than a fire escape from Hell. In fact, Peter tells us that those who fail to continue to develop in their Christian faith are shortsighted, blind, and rather forgetful of the fact that their old sinful life was a bad thing, not a good thing.

This may be one of the greatest deceptions used by Satan in the church today, responsible for the fact that we have many in our pews who make little to no effort to apply the benefits of the promises God has given in their lives. The fact that God is the Creator and Sustainer of life should mean something to us. The fact that God sent His only Son to pay for my sins should elicit a response from me. The fact that God is older than me, smarter than me, and loves me should make my life different.

Yet, in almost every survey I have read, those who claim to be Christians have no noticeable lifestyle difference from those who know nothing of Christ. In fact, there seems to be an army of so-called Christians ready to push the "legalism" button on anyone who displays any form of conviction. There seems to be a tremendous atmosphere of tolerance toward anyone who chooses to practice sin, while we subtly punish those who choose to keep their lives from being stained by the sins of this world. It seems as if almost any practice is acceptable, any entertainment is acceptable, and any form of greed is justifiable.

There is a process that should take place in the lives of believers that moves them away from themselves and their personal agendas toward God and His agenda. This process can and will be hindered by sin, so we need to identify sin, confess it, and set up our environments to minimize it.

This does not make you a legalist unless you think doing these things makes you better in God's sight or more or less acceptable. God will never love you more or less than He does right now. However, His love for you does not mean that He approves of everything you do.

Another Piece of the Truth Puzzle

There are three aspects to my salvation:

1. *Freedom from the penalty of sin (past)*
2. *Freedom from the power of sin (present)*
3. *Freedom from the presence of sin (future)*

Thought for Day 12

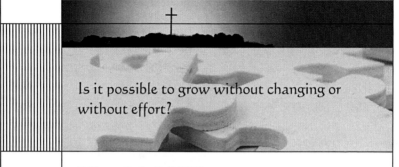

Is it possible to grow without changing or without effort?

2 Peter 1:6–9 (NLT)

6 AND KNOWLEDGE WITH SELF-CONTROL, AND SELF-CONTROL WITH PATIENT ENDURANCE, AND PATIENT ENDURANCE WITH GODLINESS,

7 AND GODLINESS WITH BROTHERLY AFFECTION, AND BROTHERLY AFFECTION WITH LOVE FOR EVERYONE.

8 THE MORE YOU GROW LIKE THIS, THE MORE PRODUCTIVE AND USEFUL YOU WILL BE IN YOUR KNOWLEDGE OF OUR LORD JESUS CHRIST.

9 BUT THOSE WHO FAIL TO DEVELOP IN THIS WAY ARE SHORTSIGHTED OR BLIND, FORGETTING THAT THEY HAVE BEEN CLEANSED FROM THEIR OLD SINS.

Satan would love for us to believe that there is no real effort in our growth, no real decision making, no real struggle. He would deceive us into believing that if we just "let go and let God," we will be fine, even if we do not know God.

The fact of the matter is that God expects us to add something to our faith. We cannot add works that would cause Him to find us more acceptable, but we can add things that will position us to see Him more clearly, and position ourselves to be used by Him.

He tells us that we should add to our faith a life of moral excellence. We should decide that we will live our lives in a manner that reflects the truth we know. We need to decide that we will be obedient in all that has been revealed to us. When we do that, we will find that God is right. You see, when I listen to God—for example, when I love my wife as Christ loved the church—I see that God is right, and in a sense I know God better, for I will have seen that He is indeed right.

As I know God better, and as I see His ways prevail, I will rededicate myself to listening to Him no matter what my human feelings or desires are. This new dedication will be tested, and when it is, I will stand firm, because I have already seen God work and am convinced of His goodness. This new spiritual endurance leads me to continue to refine my life, to refocus my life, so that I may reflect Him. As I reflect Him, I begin to love others the way I should, and become a productive plant in the garden of God.

None of this happens by accident. This productivity happens because when I came to God, I saw Him as more than just a fire escape from Hell. I saw Him as God. I realized that because He was God, and I was not, I needed to align my life with His will.

I need to continually reaffirm the fact that I will remain obedient to God no matter how I feel. Every time I do this, God's plan, purpose, and system are reaffirmed and allowed to function, and I begin once again to see that He is right, to assert my self-control, to develop my patience, and to grow in my love for others.

Growth does not happen by itself; it is deliberate, deliberative, and progressive. Have you added anything to your faith lately?

Another Piece of the Truth Puzzle

Growth demands change or it is not growth. Therefore, I should be able to measure my growth by the changes I have made. If I am not changing, I am not growing.

Thought for Day 13

I am capable of believing a lie.

2 Peter 1:10 (NLT)

10 So, dear brothers and sisters, work hard to prove that you really are among those God has called and chosen. Do these things, and you will never fall away.

One of Satan's greatest deceptions is convincing people that they are children of God when indeed they are not.

Matthew 7:22–23 (NLT)

22 On judgment day many will say to me, "Lord! Lord! We prophesied in your name and cast out demons in your name and performed many miracles in your name."

23 But I will reply, "I never knew you. Get away from me, you who break God's laws."

"On judgment day many will say . . . ." There will be many who stand before God one day who have worked in our churches, loved our children, talked the talk, and looked to us like they were walking the walk—and yet they are not a part of God's family.

This must be the greatest and cruelest deception of all, for the consequences of such a deception are beyond comprehension. Yet God says it is true. What this means is that I am capable of fooling myself. I am capable of believing a lie that was either handed to me or that I made up myself. In fact, I can imagine nothing more tragic than thinking that all is well with God and me, only to find out that I was wrong.

How do we know that we are true children of God? One indicator is the fact that our lives are in obvious transition. When we become believers, God, in the form of the Holy Spirit, lives within us and begins to convict us of our sin, and teaches us as we are in the Bible, and gives us new appetites. If we are true believers, we will see some sort of fruit or evidence of such a standing. We will see the fruit of the Spirit displayed (love, joy, peace, patience, etc.) and we will see others come to Christ because of what He is doing in our lives. We can know we're true believers as our wills begin to align with God's, as our citizenship moves from this temporal earth to our eventual eternal home. We can know we are part of God's family as we see ourselves persecuted for doing good.

There is no way I can accurately judge whether another human has truly placed his or her faith in Christ and been forgiven, but I can report that there are many who believe they are right with God when in reality they are not.

Romans 3:30 (NLT)

30 There is only one God, and he makes people right with himself only by faith, whether they are Jews or Gentiles.

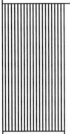

If my faith is truly in Christ as my only hope for salvation, I am a child of God. If my hope is in any other, I am deceived.

John 14:6 (NLT)

6 Jesus told him, "I am the way, the truth, and the life. No one can come to the Father except through me."

Which way are you choosing?

Ephesians 2:8–9 (NLT)

8 God saved you by his grace when you believed. And you can't take credit for this; it is a gift from God.

9 Salvation is not a reward for the good things we have done, so none of us can boast about it.

Another Piece of the Truth Puzzle

Truth must be discovered, never made up. It is found, not created. It is eternal, not temporal.

I can choose what flavor ice cream is the best, but I cannot choose what truth is and what it is not, because it already is.

Thought for Day 14

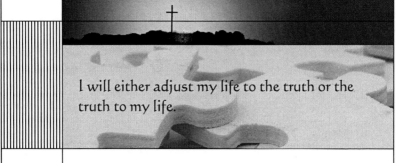

I will either adjust my life to the truth or the truth to my life.

2 Peter 2:1–3 (NLT)

1 BUT THERE WERE ALSO FALSE PROPHETS IN ISRAEL, JUST AS THERE WILL BE FALSE TEACHERS AMONG YOU. THEY WILL CLEVERLY TEACH DESTRUCTIVE HERESIES AND EVEN DENY THE MASTER WHO BOUGHT THEM. IN THIS WAY, THEY WILL BRING SUDDEN DESTRUCTION ON THEMSELVES.

2 MANY WILL FOLLOW THEIR EVIL TEACHING AND SHAMEFUL IMMORALITY. AND BECAUSE OF THESE TEACHERS, THE WAY OF TRUTH WILL BE SLANDERED.

3 IN THEIR GREED THEY WILL MAKE UP CLEVER LIES TO GET HOLD OF YOUR MONEY. BUT GOD CONDEMNED THEM LONG AGO, AND THEIR DESTRUCTION WILL NOT BE DELAYED.

Today the influence of the media grips the modern world. There is much in the media that is acceptable, yet there is much that is totally unacceptable. For one who loves God to sit and be entertained by the very things that break His heart is not right.

One of the definitive remarks concerning the identification of false teachers has to do with the cleverness of how they introduce destructive heresies. There will be those who follow these teachers and live lives of shameful immorality. The cleverest smokescreen may

be the one raised by those who claim that anyone who avoids all immorality is a legalist, or cannot relate to the world.

How much immorality should be acceptable to us? What should the standard be for those who love God? Does it matter that the money we spend on entertainment ends up promoting causes that break the King's heart? Does it matter if we have a little immorality in our lives?

How much faithfulness should a wife expect from a husband? If a man is 90 percent faithful, is that good enough? Can a husband watch just a little pornography? Can I cheat just 5 percent on my taxes?

If I opened my life to all for inspection, would they be able to follow everything I do to excess, and love God and people more because of it, or would some of the things I have allowed, justified, and even teach by my life be destructive to God and His purposes in their lives?

The entertainment industry is based on greed. Television sponsors are continually trying to get me to buy something I do not need, and they have many ways of making me feel as if I am constantly on the outside looking in. Is this an industry I should support in any way, shape, or form?

False teachers slander absolutes and discourage people from being completely pure, while doing what they must to gain people's loyalty for personal gain. This is not good, and will end up being disastrous both for the leader and for those who follow such a leader.

What is our ministry all about? Do we talk with and work with people to squeeze money out of them, or because we want them to walk intimately with God?

Another Piece of the Truth Puzzle

One day, I will be surprised by truth or I will be confirmed by it. Which will it be?

_____

_____

_____

_____

_____

_____

_____

_____

_____

_____

_____

_____

_____

_____

_____

_____

_____

_____

Thought for Day 15

I am on a path toward something.

2 Peter 2:5–8 (NLT)

5 And God did not spare the ancient world—except for Noah and the seven others in his family. Noah warned the world of God's righteous judgment. So God protected Noah when he destroyed the world of ungodly people with a vast flood.

6 Later, God condemned the cities of Sodom and Gomorrah and turned them into heaps of ashes. He made them an example of what will happen to ungodly people.

7 But God also rescued Lot out of Sodom because he was a righteous man who was sick of the shameful immorality of the wicked people around him.

8 Yes, Lot was a righteous man who was tormented in his soul by the wickedness he saw and heard day after day.

But God rescued Lot, a "righteous man"? This is the last mention of Lot in Scripture. How could he be considered a righteous man? Is this not the man who lived in Sodom, who offered his daughters to be raped, whose wife was

turned into a pillar of salt? Are we talking about the same man? Yes.

It is quite reassuring that God remembers the good about a man, and not necessarily all of the evil we participate in. God always seems to refer to David as a man after His own heart, whereas I remember David as a man lusting after Bathsheba, a murderer, and a liar. I need to take time to thank God for His selective memory.

I also need to see how a man like Lot got himself into such a bad situation. I am certain that he did not wake up one morning and decide to be on the wrong side of the tracks. There must have been a process that he followed, an apparently acceptable path that led to destruction.

If you look at the story of Lot, found in Genesis chapter 13, you will see some very troubling decisions that eventually led to his undoing. First and foremost, when his and Abram's herds grew and needed to be separated, Lot chose the best land for himself and gave Abram what was left. He then went on to pitch his tent toward Sodom (he probably was appalled by the idea of living in such a godless city). Soon, though, he was living in Sodom, and apparently became one of the leaders of the city.

The Bible is not clear as to how he got from pitching his tent to leading the city, but says that he did so. I suspect that the environment he set up allowed him to view the city, to watch the fun, to be entertained by what entertained them. I imagine that he might have taken some day trips into town to check out the merchants, and possibly saw some real estate that was more desirable than a tent. He probably moved in and saw opportunities to

lead, to help the city reform, and took advantage of such a wonderful blessing, *obviously* from God.

That is, he took advantage of these "wonderful blessings" until one day God had had enough. It was on that day that we saw the depths to which Lot had fallen. As Genesis 19 tells us, he would soon lose his home, lose his wife, and have his daughters trick him into incest. Life was not what he hoped for, yet, in all of this, God saw through the bad decisions to a heart that was, at least at the end, disgusted with the sin that was so evident. God is gracious but just.

What decisions have you made that have turned you toward Sodom? What do you need to do to change your course while there is still time?

Another Piece of the Truth Puzzle

The path I am on today is leading me to some destination. If I adjust my path, I will alter my destination.

Thought for Day 16

There is no such thing as a secret life.

2 Peter 2:14 (NLT)

14 They commit adultery with their eyes, and their desire for sin is never satisfied. They lure unstable people into sin, and they are well trained in greed. They live under God's curse.

Peter continues to talk about characteristics of the false teachers, the deceivers. He tells us that they are not necessarily the ones who are overtly committing sexually depraved acts, but they are committing adultery with their eyes, and never really seem to be satisfied with the sin they so enjoy.

Pornography is a primary example of sin that has gripped our nation. There are millions of child porn sites, all illegal but available to anyone who has a computer and a connection to the Internet. Clothing styles for women are often designed to grab men's attention. Television programs, advertising, and a continual onslaught of spam e-mails underscore the importance of the sexual and the erotic.

This problem is not new in our culture, or in any culture, but it is a major problem among those who want to be leaders, for they continue to dabble in a supposedly private world, satisfying their lustful eyes, while hoping and praying that God will bless their ministry.

Satan knows the tremendous temptation that the lust of the eyes presents to the leader, and he will do whatever is necessary to keep reminding us of what is available out there. Therefore, we must agree with God that we are subject to such temptations and be deliberate about setting up our environments so that this temptation cannot overcome us.

The problem will never be entirely solved, because too many people are involved in the problem. From the time our daughters are young, they look forward to wearing clothes that make men notice them. They cannot wait for the time they can dress up, make men drool, have dad tell them how beautiful they are, and head to the dance floor and move to the music in ways that scream, "Look at me, look at my body, look at how I move." Moms seem to take great pride in this, and dads love the fact that their daughters are so beautiful. Men, in the privacy of their offices, enjoy a little pornography now and then, and take their wives or girlfriends to movies full of sex and violence. The appetite for sexual pleasure starts with the eyes, so all this visual stimulation is headed in a specific and dangerous direction.

The deception comes when we think we can handle these live coals and not be burnt. The deception comes when Christian girls want to be like the others, the godless girls, who live to have men desire their bodies. We do not want our Christian daughters to not fit in or to be strange, so we encourage them to be safe and participate without causing such lusting to take place. We ask them to hold live coals in their bosom and not get burnt.

Our country has a drinking problem, but we will not deal with it, because we like to drink. We have an obesity problem, but we will not deal with it, because we like to eat and do not like to exercise. We have a sexual problem, but we will not deal with it, because we like to satisfy our sexual fantasies.

What is it you're not dealing with, and why?

Another Piece of the Truth Puzzle

I have never had a private moment.

_____

_____

_____

_____

_____

_____

_____

_____

_____

_____

_____

Thought for Day 17

Something will control me today.

2 Peter 2:19 (NLT)

19 THEY PROMISE FREEDOM, BUT THEY THEMSELVES ARE SLAVES OF SIN AND CORRUPTION. FOR YOU ARE A SLAVE TO WHATEVER CONTROLS YOU.

I am a slave to whatever controls me. What is it that controls me? What *should* control me?

I could be very pious and claim that God controls me. In reality, though, I am often controlled by my appetites—my appetite for power, or pleasure, or food, or acceptance. Appetites can be so powerful that they lead you to do all sorts of evil things.

A few years ago I was told that I had had a heart attack. After talking with the cardiologist, I agreed to modify my diet. I was not modifying my diet because my appetites had changed; I was modifying my diet because I needed to, or I would risk another heart attack.

The trouble with this diet, as well as other diets, is that it restricted some foods that I found very desirable. Some of the foods that I used to eat in abundance, I now needed to limit or totally eliminate from my regular diet.

In the beginning, I found that eating the right foods was difficult, but I remained on track because I believed this

doctor knew what he was talking about, and I was afraid of having another heart attack.

I've now been on this restricted diet for years. I have lost about 40 pounds, feel great, exercise regularly, and can honestly say that I have little to no desire for the foods that once so captivated me. In fact, I now have a whole new set of appetites that include foods that help heal and protect my cardiovascular system.

How did I get to this point? First and foremost, I had a crisis: a heart attack. Second, I knew that in the crisis there was one who knew the best route to both repair and prevention. Third, I adjusted my environment so that the foods on the "acceptable" list were the foods that were available.

I see the same thing happening in my spiritual life. Before I can really begin to develop habits that will help heal and protect, I need to admit that I have a problem—a problem with sin. Then I need to go to the One who can help me cure this problem, the One who really knows, the One who is an expert on sinlessness.

From there on, I need to arrange my environment so that it is conducive to producing the end result that I desire. This means that there are some things that need to go, some things I will no longer buy, some things that I may never touch, see, or listen to again. As I go through this process, I begin to feel a new spiritual freedom. I am no longer controlled by my passions and desires. I am con-trolled by a deliberate decision to surround myself with the things that will promote spiritual health. Just as in the physical world, what starts as an act of obedience soon becomes the habit of a successful life.

What environmental changes do you need to make? Will you wait until the crisis to make those changes?

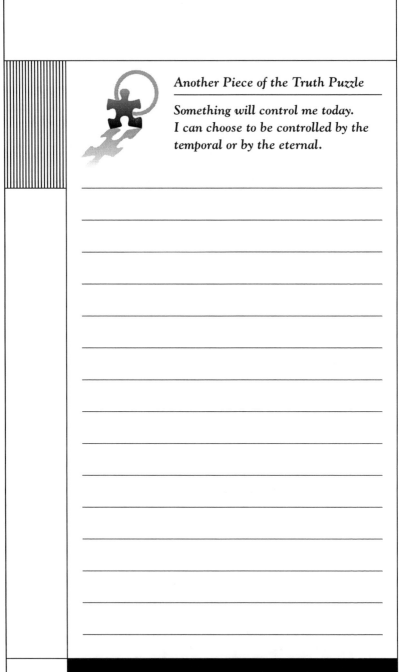

Another Piece of the Truth Puzzle

Something will control me today.
I can choose to be controlled by the
temporal or by the eternal.

Thought for Day 18

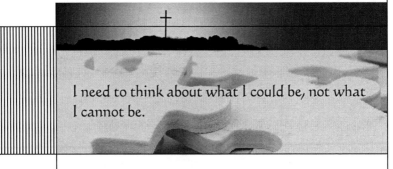

I need to think about what I could be, not what I cannot be.

2 Peter 2:20–22 (NLT)

20 And when people escape from the wickedness of the world by knowing our Lord and Savior Jesus Christ and then get tangled up and enslaved by sin again, they are worse off than before.

21 It would be better if they had never known the way to righteousness than to know it and then reject the command they were given to live a holy life.

22 They prove the truth of this proverb: "A dog returns to its vomit." And another says, "A washed pig returns to the mud."

How bad is it to have success within your grasp and let it go?

God has not saved us just to keep us from Hell. He has saved us unto good works. These good works are not a condition for our salvation, but they are a condition for a successful life.

God, the Creator, the Designer, the Lover of man, has given us all the instructions we need to live a godly life. If we choose to ignore what He says, what hope do we have?

When I was young, I was on the high school swim team. I was not much of a swimmer at first, but due to some physical limitations, swimming was the only sport in which I could participate. I thought it would be easy because my brother, who was older than I, was a star swimmer. I was sure that great swimming ability was in the genes, and I attacked the sport with all the gusto of a new recruit.

During my first meet, I remember swimming a hundred-yard sprint. This meant we had to swim four lengths of the pool. I was nervous, but I glanced at my coach and at my brother, took my place on the blocks, and took off with the gun.

Well, that was my last pleasant thought during that race; all my competition was done with the race and out of the pool before I was finished with my third lap. As I took my breaths, I saw people in the stands pointing and laughing. I felt humiliated, defeated, and worthless.

Then, all of a sudden, my brother and my coach got in between my view of the jeerers and became my cheerers. I finished the race and was consoled by these two men. From that day on, I dedicated myself to not letting those two down. I practiced, swam, and did whatever it took to win, and win I did; my second year was an unbelievable success. These two men forced me to see what I could be. They got between me and the crowd, and forced me to deal with the defeat, but in a way that propelled me toward being my best. I did not want to go back to being that loser again.

When I became a believer, God stepped in between me and the world. He made sure I understood where I currently was, but always showed me where I could be. Why would I ever want to go back to where I had been?

How bad would it be for me to go back to the level of that first performance after four years of competitive training and swimming? It would be the ultimate agony of defeat.

Do you understand what you could be? Could you ever be satisfied again with where you once were?

Another Piece of the Truth Puzzle

Christianity is defined by what Christ did for me, by His provision at the cross. My Christian life should be defined by what I do, not by what I do not do.

_____

_____

_____

_____

_____

_____

_____

_____

_____

Thought for Day 19

Selective memory can be both good and bad.

2 Peter 3:1–2 (NLT)

1 THIS IS MY SECOND LETTER TO YOU, DEAR FRIENDS, AND IN BOTH OF THEM I HAVE TRIED TO STIMULATE YOUR WHOLESOME THINKING AND REFRESH YOUR MEMORY.

2 I WANT YOU TO REMEMBER WHAT THE HOLY PROPHETS SAID LONG AGO AND WHAT OUR LORD AND SAVIOR COMMANDED THROUGH YOUR APOSTLES.

Why is it so easy to forget?

One of the evil one's great deceptions is to make me think that once I know something, I know something. That is just not true. In fact, I often know something and then realize that I don't really know what I thought I knew! (Are you with me here?)

I tell you that I know I should exercise on a regular basis, but there are times when I do not exercise on a regular basis. Often I have to be reminded of what I need to do.

God's Word tells me that I need to pray without ceasing, and I need to meditate on His Word day and night. Why?

Why can't I just read it, take the test, and be done with it?

Could it be because it is living?

Hebrews 4:12 (NLT)

12 For the word of God is alive and powerful. It is sharper than the sharpest two-edged sword, cutting between soul and spirit, between joint and marrow. It exposes our innermost thoughts and desires.

The Bible is living. It is able to attack my bad thoughts, my poorly conceived ideas, and keep me clean and on track. Because my thoughts are forever in motion, I must constantly check them against the Word of God.

God, throughout history, has seemed to love placing reminders in front of people so that they will never forget the obvious; this recognizes the fact that I can indeed forget the obvious.

I think that every man should have a picture of his wife and family in a frame that has the words "No Regrets" engraved on it. I think he should look at that picture every time he leaves the office, and every time he returns, and remind himself of the fact that he is to be faithful to his wife, and a leader to his household. I have that phrase plastered everywhere in my life, for when the day comes that I close my eyes on this life, I want to know that I have been to my family what I should have been, and that I have accomplished the purpose God created me to accomplish.

This will not happen by mistake or by accident.

What reminders do you have surrounding you each day? Are you totally surrounded by sports memorabilia, pictures of mountains, or cars? What should you have in your life as reminders, and what should you be reminded of?

Those who minimize their reminders minimize their ability to achieve the goal.

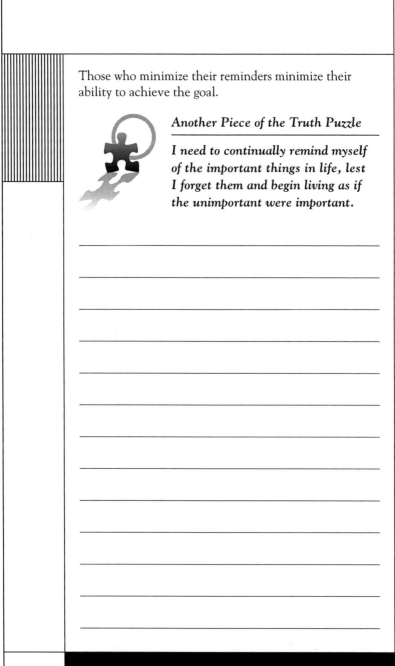

Another Piece of the Truth Puzzle

I need to continually remind myself of the important things in life, lest I forget them and begin living as if the unimportant were important.

_____

_____

_____

_____

_____

_____

_____

_____

_____

_____

_____

_____

_____

_____

Thought for Day 20

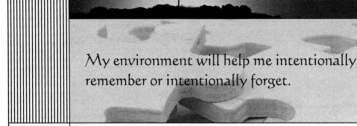

My environment will help me intentionally remember or intentionally forget.

2 Peter 3:5–7 (NLT)

5 THEY DELIBERATELY FORGET THAT GOD MADE THE HEAVENS BY THE WORD OF HIS COMMAND, AND HE BROUGHT THE EARTH OUT FROM THE WATER AND SURROUNDED IT WITH WATER.

6 THEN HE USED THE WATER TO DESTROY THE ANCIENT WORLD WITH A MIGHTY FLOOD.

7 AND BY THE SAME WORD, THE PRESENT HEAVENS AND EARTH HAVE BEEN STORED UP FOR FIRE. THEY ARE BEING KEPT FOR THE DAY OF JUDGMENT, WHEN UNGODLY PEOPLE WILL BE DESTROYED.

Wow, who would deliberately forget that God is the Creator?

What is the significance of deliberately forgetting that God made all that was made?

Well, it certainly makes life easier if I do not need to answer to anyone. If there is not a Creator, there will be no judgment, there are no expectations, and there is no real plan. If all things are accidental, I can live like an accident and do whatever I want whenever I want.

If God is the Creator, then God has a plan. If He has a plan, I am either a part of it or not a part of it. That may be pressure I do not want.

What happens, if I refuse to remember God as the Creator and Sustainer of all life, is that I begin to elevate *my* ways and *my* thinking. I begin to propagate the greatest deception of all: the idea that I am the be-all and end of all things.

Lucifer was one who seemed to forget the fact that he was not the Creator, but one who was created. He longed to take on God's role and God's responsibilities. Lucifer was less than satisfied with the spot in the universe God gave to him, and he began to lobby God and others to achieve his personal advancement.

When Lucifer showed up in the garden, he used the same thinking to persuade Eve and Adam to sin. He told them that their lives would be better, that they would know more, and that they were missing out by listening to God.

Satan was wrong.

He is *still* wrong.

One day, Satan will be punished for eternity for his attitude and his evil. In fact, all those who choose to ignore the fact that God created the world, and who refuse to subject themselves to Him and His ways, will be recipients of God's wrath.

As I am reminded that God is the Creator, I am also reminded that I am the created. As I remind myself that He is the Sustainer, I am reminded that I am one who needs sustaining. As I am reminded of God's creativity, I am reminded that I am nothing without Him.

These are good reminders that will pay rich dividends in life and in the hereafter.

What reminders do you have in your life of the fact that God is the Creator and Sustainer of life? Does this really matter to you?

Another Piece of the Truth Puzzle

Environment does not cause growth; it helps or hinders growth, but is never the cause.

Thought for Day 21

My death is certain. My life on earth is not certain.

2 Peter 3:8–13 (NLT)

8 BUT YOU MUST NOT FORGET THIS ONE THING, DEAR FRIENDS: A DAY IS LIKE A THOUSAND YEARS TO THE LORD, AND A THOUSAND YEARS IS LIKE A DAY.

9 THE LORD ISN'T REALLY BEING SLOW ABOUT HIS PROMISE, AS SOME PEOPLE THINK. NO, HE IS BEING PATIENT FOR YOUR SAKE. HE DOES NOT WANT ANYONE TO BE DESTROYED, BUT WANTS EVERYONE TO REPENT.

10 BUT THE DAY OF THE LORD WILL COME AS UNEXPECT-EDLY AS A THIEF. THEN THE HEAVENS WILL PASS AWAY WITH A TERRIBLE NOISE, AND THE VERY ELEMENTS THEM-SELVES WILL DISAPPEAR IN FIRE, AND THE EARTH AND EVERYTHING ON IT WILL BE FOUND TO DESERVE JUDGMENT.

11 SINCE EVERYTHING AROUND US IS GOING TO BE DESTROYED LIKE THIS, WHAT HOLY AND GODLY LIVES YOU SHOULD LIVE,

12 LOOKING FORWARD TO THE DAY OF GOD AND HURRYING IT ALONG. ON THAT DAY, HE WILL SET THE HEAVENS ON FIRE, AND THE ELEMENTS WILL MELT AWAY IN THE FLAMES.

13 BUT WE ARE LOOKING FORWARD TO THE NEW HEAVENS AND NEW EARTH HE HAS PROMISED, A WORLD FILLED WITH GOD'S RIGHTEOUSNESS.

Another great deception passed over on us by the evil one is the idea that life will always go on as we know it today. We are told over and over again in Scripture that this life we know will one day end. The timing of the end is not given, but the fact of the end is quite clear.

Because we have made this world our home, we do not often like talking about its eventual destruction. Take a moment and look around the room you are in now. Take a moment to imagine it all gone, vaporized in a moment. Think of the moment when you will stand before God and how much of what you invested your life in will be with you.

As we saw earlier, it is important that we see God as both the Creator and the Sustainer. The very atoms that are currently held together could, at any time God chooses, disorganize, split, and cause an explosion that will result in a nothingness beyond our imaginations.

I can only imagine God sitting in heaven watching our activities and wondering why we spend so much time and energy on things that He will one day destroy. I can imagine Him being puzzled by the way we think, by our short-sightedness, and by what we call our investment strategies.

How would I spend my time and resources if I were thinking of things as God thought of things? Am I really living in reality, or have I been deceived into believing that the temporal is not temporal?

What God says is true. Therefore, I need to rethink my investment strategy. It would be most wise to take as much with me to eternity as I can, yet there is nothing on this earth apart from people that I can take with me. What shall I do while I wait? Peter tells me plainly.

Peter 3:14 (NLT)

14 AND SO, DEAR FRIENDS, WHILE YOU ARE WAITING FOR THESE THINGS TO HAPPEN, MAKE EVERY EFFORT TO BE FOUND LIVING PEACEFUL LIVES THAT ARE PURE AND BLAMELESS IN HIS SIGHT.

Will God say that I lived a pure and blameless life? There is still time . . . for now.

Another Piece of the Truth Puzzle

My death is more certain than my life.

Final Thoughts

Things alter for the worse spontaneously, if they be not altered for the better designedly. (Bacon)

It is easy to believe what I believe because I already believe it. I like who I am and what I believe, and can defend it with sound thoughts and rhetoric. The problem with that is that my sound thought and decent rhetoric do not necessarily constitute truth.

Herein lies the problem of all humankind. We can think, talk, and conclude whatever we want and still be thinking wrongly, talking wrongly, and concluding wrongly. We can surround ourselves with intellectuals, theologians, and scientists, and still live in ignorance. We can listen to talk radio, news shows, and read the nation's major newspapers, and still live in deception. We can go to the best schools and seminaries, and still live our lives in ignorance and foolishness.

The only way to know that we are not living in deception is to know and be obedient to God. I need not understand Him. I need not agree with Him. I need no further explanation from Him than what He has already revealed. I do need to realize that God has given me enough information to satisfy my faith, but never to satisfy my curiosity.

My proper response to the truth in God's Word will always be obedience. God is God, I am Dave, and no other arrangement is possible. This means that truth will be something Dave needs to discover, not make up.

Truth is something that belongs to God and is revealed to Dave. Truth is something by which I should evaluate my life, rather than using my life to evaluate truth.

I hope that all who have journeyed through this book will begin to develop the habits of asking God to reveal to them the truth of His Word and the errors of our ways. We need to see a new generation of soldiers for our King who are more interested in the orders of the King than the comforts of the Kingdom. We need to see deception as the grand enemy, and do whatever is needed to live in the truth.

Satan's greatest weapon is deception. If that weapon is rendered useless, his efforts will be in vain, and all those who have honestly evaluated their lives and lived in the truth will rejoice!

There is an end to this thing we call life. There will be winners and losers. There will be those who are proven right and those who are proven wrong. On which side will you land? How do you know for sure?

Revelation 19:20 (NLT)

20 AND THE BEAST WAS CAPTURED, AND WITH HIM THE FALSE PROPHET WHO DID MIGHTY MIRACLES ON BEHALF OF THE BEAST—MIRACLES THAT DECEIVED ALL WHO HAD ACCEPTED THE MARK OF THE BEAST AND WHO WORSHIPED HIS STATUE. BOTH THE BEAST AND HIS FALSE PROPHET WERE THROWN ALIVE INTO THE FIERY LAKE OF BURNING SULFUR.

In the end, God wins. All who willingly followed Satan and all who were deceived lose. That will be the beginning of the end.

1 Corinthians 15:58 (NLT)

58 So, my dear brothers and sisters, be strong and immovable. Always work enthusiastically for the Lord, for you know that nothing you do for the Lord is ever useless.

Silver Birch Ranch
"To Know Christ and To Make Him Known"

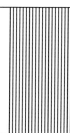

Silver Birch Ranch has been serving our nation's youth since the summer of 1968. Its unique location allows children and families to enjoy swimming, horseback riding, white water rafting and more, while being challenged to understand and respond to God's plan for their lives.

Silver Birch Ranch also hosts year-round conferences and retreats for churches, and a Bible college, the Nicolet Bible Institute.

Silver Birch Ranch has many materials to help you in your effort to be intimate with God and family. Through the Omega Force program, you can receive materials that will help you with your personal walk with God, and remind you to live your life with "no regrets."

For information about Silver Birch Ranch, Nicolet Bible Institute, and the Omega Force program, please visit our web site at www.silverbirchranch.org.

If you are interested in inviting Dave Wager as a speaker for your special event, please contact him at Silver Birch Ranch, N6120 Sawyer Lake Road, White Lake, WI 54491, or by email at dave.wager@silverbirchranch.org.